Great Inventions

THE AUTOMOBILE

by Julie L. Sinclair

Consultant:

Jim Higham
Manager, Auto Collection
"Tin Lizzie" Auto Museum Inc.
Winnipeg, Manitoba

Capstone press

Mankato, Minnesota

Fact Finders is published by Capstone Press
151 Good Counsel Drive, P.O. Box 669, Mankato, Minnesota 56002
http://www.capstone-press.com

Library of Congress Cataloging-in-Publication Data
Sinclair, Julie L.
    The automobile / Julie L. Sinclair.
    p. cm.—(Fact finders. Great inventions)
    Includes bibliographical references (p. 31) and index.
    Contents: Ford and the machine—Before the automobile—Inventors—How an automobile works—The world begins to drive—Automobiles today.
    ISBN 0-7368-2214-3 (hardcover)
    1. Automobiles—History—Juvenile literature. [1. Automobiles—History.] I. Title. II. Series.
TL147 .S563 2004
629.222'09—dc21   2002156500

Editorial Credits
Roberta Schmidt, editor; Juliette Peters, series designer and illustrator; Alta Schaffer, photo researcher; Eric Kudalis, product planning editor

Photo Credits
Comstock, 24–25
Corbis/Bettmann, cover, 13, 23, 26 (left); Paul C. Chauncey, 14–15
Hulton/Archive Photos by Getty Images, 5, 8, 9, 10–11, 12, 19, 20–21; Museum of the City of New York/Jacob A. Riis, 6–7
John J. Blowers and Wanda Rolfing, 27 (middle)
North Wind Picture Archives, 22
Stock Montage Inc., 26 (middle)
Thomas J. & Betty Ann Egan, 1, 27 (right)
Tomm Wells, 27 (left)
Wenatcheecars.com, 26 (right)

Table of Contents

Chapter 1

Ford and the Machine

In 1879, a 16-year-old boy set out on an adventure. Henry Ford left his family and farm near Dearborn, Michigan. He traveled alone to the big city of Detroit. He wanted to work on machines.

Ford spent many years working on an automobile. The automobile was a new machine at the time. Ford wanted to make it better. He worked for many years in a shed behind his house. In 1896, he drove out of the shed in his first automobile.

Henry Ford finished his first automobile in 1896. He called it the "Quadricycle."

FIRST · CAR

Ford wanted to build automobiles that anyone could buy. In 1903, he started the Ford Motor Company. Because of Ford and his company, millions of people were able to buy automobiles.

Chapter 2

Before the Automobile

In the 1800s, people did not travel very far from home. Most people did not travel more than 1,200 miles (1,900 kilometers) in their lifetimes.

Traveling was not easy in those days. Few roads existed. Most roads were dirt paths. When it rained, the dirt became mud. Traveling on these roads was messy.

In the 1800s, muddy roads made traveling messy and difficult.

Stagecoaches were a common way of traveling in the 1800s.

Most people walked or rode horses. They also rode in wagons or carriages pulled by horses. These ways of traveling were slow. Horses could get tired and sick. They needed rest, food, and water.

In the 1800s, people also traveled on trains. Trains made traveling easier. Trains did not need rest or food. They could carry many people at a time.

Until 1886, train companies could make their tracks as narrow or as wide as they wanted.

Before the automobile, people traveled on trains.

But trains could not go everywhere people wanted to go. Trains could go only where there were railroad tracks. Riding the train also cost a lot of money.

People searched for new ways to travel. Some people wanted to fly through the air. Other people wanted to drive a wagon that could move without horses.

Inventors

Many people tried to build machines that moved by themselves. Their work helped develop the first automobiles.

Early Inventors

In 1769, Nicolas-Joseph Cugnot designed the first vehicle to move by its own power. Cugnot's vehicle had three wheels. It was powered by a steam engine. But the steam engine did not work very well. The vehicle had to stop every 10 to 15 minutes to build up power.

Cugnot's vehicle was difficult to control. When it ran into a garden wall, it had the first motor accident in history.

Gottlieb Daimler was a German engineer and inventor.

In the 1830s, some inventors built automobiles powered by electric motors. These vehicles could reach speeds of 10 to 20 miles (16 to 32 kilometers) per hour. But they could not go very far. They usually ran out of power after 50 miles (80 kilometers).

In the 1870s, two German engineers found another way to power a vehicle. Nicolaus August Otto and Gottlieb Daimler built an engine that ran on gasoline. This engine was called the "Otto cycle engine." It became the power source for most automobiles.

In 1885, Karl Benz made the first modern automobile. He built an engine like the Otto cycle engine. He put it on a three-wheeled carriage.

The next year, Daimler put the Otto cycle engine on a four-wheeled stagecoach. Daimler's invention was the first four-wheeled motor car in history.

Benz's three-wheeled carriage was the first modern automobile.

Chapter 4

How an Automobile Works

Today's automobiles are made of almost 14,000 parts. All of these parts make cars safe and easy to drive.

The Internal Combustion Gasoline Engine

Most cars today use an engine like the Otto cycle engine. It is called an internal combustion gasoline engine.

The internal combustion engine burns a mixture of fuel and air. The mixture makes hot gases in the engine.

An automobile is often called a "car." This word refers to any vehicle that moves on wheels. You can find the word "car" in "carriage" and "railroad car."

A mechanic makes sure that all of a car's parts work correctly.

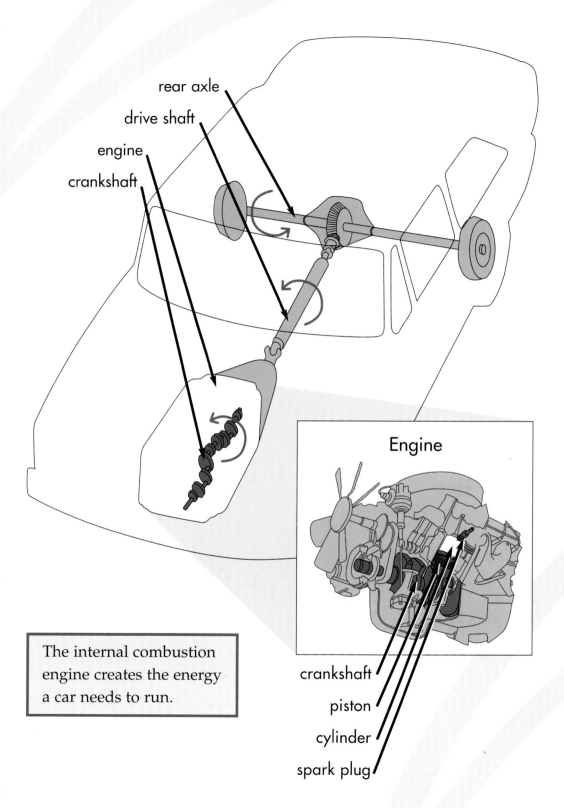

rear axle

drive shaft

engine

crankshaft

Engine

crankshaft

piston

cylinder

spark plug

The internal combustion engine creates the energy a car needs to run.

Sparks from the engine's spark plugs make the gases explode. These explosions make the engine's pistons move up and down inside tubes called cylinders. The pistons move up and down about 6,000 times each minute. The pistons are connected to the crankshaft. This zigzag-shaped rod turns the driveshaft. The driveshaft spins the axle. The axle makes the wheels of the car turn.

Important Car Systems

Each car also has an electrical system, a steering system, a braking system, and a suspension system. The electrical system controls all parts of the car that need electricity. The steering and braking systems make the car turn and stop. The suspension system makes the car drive smoothly.

Chapter 5

The World Begins to Drive

In the late 1800s, many people became interested in automobiles. Companies around the world started to build and sell cars.

In 1893, Charles and Frank Duryea built the first gasoline-powered automobile in the United States. These brothers were bicycle makers. But they knew people would want automobiles more than bicycles.

By 1900, 50 companies in the United States were building automobiles. Gasoline automobiles soon outsold all other types of vehicles.

Panhard & Levassor was the first company to build automobiles. This company started in France in 1889.

In 1904, cars from all over the country joined in an automobile tour to the World's Fair at St. Louis, Missouri.

In the early years, building an automobile was slow, hard work. Workers made one car at a time. Each automobile was made by hand.

Because making a car took so long, companies made people pay a lot for cars. Most people did not make enough money to buy one.

Mass Production

Ransom E. Olds helped build cars faster. His workers wheeled a cart of car parts to each car frame. More than one car then could be made at a time. By building cars faster, Olds helped lower the cost of cars.

Ford's most famous car was the Model T. By 1927, Ford's company had built more than 15 million Model Ts.

In 1913, Henry Ford did
more to speed up car-making.
He used a moving assembly
line. Ford put a car frame on
a moving track. Workers
stood beside the track. Each
worker added one piece
to the frame as it passed.
When the car reached the end
of the line, it was complete.

The moving assembly line
made Ford and his company
famous. It also made the cost
of building a car go down.
When the price went down,
more people were able to
buy cars.

The moving assembly line made
car-making faster and easier.

Automobiles created the need for better roads.

The first mile (1.6 kilometers) of concrete highway was laid in Wayne County, Michigan, in 1909.

The Automobile Changes America

Cars needed better roads than horses did. Car drivers also did not like dirty, muddy roads. They wanted concrete roads. In 1916, U.S. President Woodrow Wilson signed the Federal Road Act. This law set up a national highway system to take care of roads.

The automobile gave people more freedom. Cars made traveling easy and fast. People could live farther away from their jobs. People began to build homes outside of cities.

The automobile led to many new businesses. People with cars needed gas stations. They needed shops to fix their cars. Drive-in restaurants and movie theaters appeared in the 1930s and 1940s.

The car also led to new laws. By the early 1900s, many states had speed limit and driver's license laws.

Drive-in theaters were one of the many businesses created to serve automobile owners.

Chapter 6

Automobiles Today

Henry Ford's moving assembly line started the automobile age. By 1929, U.S. car companies were making more than 5 million automobiles each year.

In the mid-1900s, many different types of cars became popular. Europeans began to build small cars that cost less money. American carmakers built larger cars with many special features.

By 1965, more than 77 percent of American families owned automobiles. People throughout the world owned more than 98 million cars.

The large number of cars on the roads today can cause traffic problems.

More than 600 million motor vehicles are in the world today. One-third of these vehicles are in the United States.

Carmakers today are looking for ways to build better cars. They want to make cars that can go farther and use less gasoline. Carmakers also want to build cars that do not pollute the air.

Automobiles through the Years

Duryea automobile

1893

Ford Model T

1923

Ford Coupe

1936

Today, the average adult American travels almost 12,000 miles (19,000 kilometers) each year by car.

People have already built cars with motors that are powered by sunlight, electricity, or other fuels. Companies continue to improve these motors.

Automobiles are an important part of life for many people. They make traveling fast and easy.

Cadillac Coupe De Ville

1959

Chevrolet Monte Carlo

1979

Toyota Prius

2002

Fast Facts

- Before the automobile, most people traveled by **horse** or by **train**.

- **Nicolas-Joseph Cugnot** built the first vehicle to move by its own power in 1769.

- **Karl Benz** built the first modern automobile in 1885.

- In 1913, Henry Ford's company used a **moving assembly line** to speed up the car-making process.

- **The automobile** led to the creation of new roads, new stores, and new laws.

- There are almost **500 million motor vehicles** in the world today.

- Cars can be powered by **engines** that run on steam, electricity, gasoline, or other fuels. The gasoline engine is the most common engine, but it produces pollution.

Hands On:

Talk about Car Parts

Cars have many parts that help people drive safely. The next time you are in a car with an adult, look for these parts. Talk about how each part helps the driver.

Turn signals—Turn signals tell other drivers when the car will be turning either left or right. There are turn signals on both sides of the car and in the front and the back.

Headlights—Headlights help the driver to see the road. They also help other people see the car.

Windshield wipers—Windshield wipers clear off the windshield when it is raining or snowing. The driver would not be able to see through the rain or snow without windshield wipers.

Gas gauge—The gas gauge tells the driver how much fuel is in the gas tank. If there is no gas in the tank, the car will not run.

Odometer—The odometer keeps track of how many miles or kilometers the car has been driven.

Speedometer—The speedometer shows the driver how fast the car is going. The driver must be careful to follow speed limit laws.

Glossary

assembly line (uh-SEM-blee LINE)—an arrangement of machines and workers in a factory; on an assembly line, work passes from one person or machine to the next until the work is complete.

engineer (en-juh-NIHR)—someone who designs or builds machines

internal combustion engine (in-TUR-nuhl kuhm-BUSS-chuhn EN-juhn)—an engine that gets power by burning fuel

inventor (in–VEN-tuhr)—someone who makes something new

pollute (puh-LOOT)—to make dirty

steam engine (STEEM EN-juhn)—an engine that gets power by heating water to make steam

vehicle (VEE-uh-kuhl)—a machine that carries people and goods

Internet Sites

Do you want to find out more about the automobile?
Let FactHound, our fact-finding hound dog, do the research for you.

Here's how:
1) Visit *http://www.facthound.com*
2) Type in the **Book ID** number:
   0736822143
3) Click on **FETCH IT**.

FactHound will fetch Internet sites picked by our editors just for you!

Read More

Bankston, John. *Henry Ford and the Assembly Line.* Unlocking the Secrets of Science. Bear, Del.: Mitchell Lane, 2002.

Dooling, Michael. *The Great Horseless Carriage Race.* New York: Holiday House, 2002.

Ford, Carin T. *Henry Ford: The Car Man.* Famous Inventors. Berkeley Heights, N.J.: Enslow, 2003.

Index